ZRjC
8/11

DOGS SET I

MUTTS

Heidi Mathea

ABDO Publishing Company

visit us at
www.abdopublishing.com

Published by ABDO Publishing Company, 8000 West 78th Street, Edina, Minnesota 55439. Copyright © 2011 by Abdo Consulting Group, Inc. International copyrights reserved in all countries. No part of this book may be reproduced in any form without written permission from the publisher. The Checkerboard Library™ is a trademark and logo of ABDO Publishing Company.

Printed in the United States of America, North Mankato, Minnesota.
042010
092010

 PRINTED ON RECYCLED PAPER

Cover Photo: Peter Arnold
Interior Photos: Corbis pp. 7, 15; Getty Images pp. 9, 11, 12, 14, 21; iStockphoto p. 13; Peter Arnold p. 5; Photolibrary pp. 17, 19

Editor: Tamara L. Britton
Art Direction & Cover Design: Neil Klinepier

Library of Congress Cataloging-in-Publication Data

Mathea, Heidi, 1979-
  Mutts / Heidi Mathea.
       p. cm. -- (Dogs)
  Includes index.
  ISBN 978-1-61613-408-2
  1. Mutts (Dogs)--Juvenile literature. I. Title.
  SF426.5.M278 2011
  636.7--dc22
                                        2010013417

CONTENTS

THE DOG FAMILY

For more than 12,000 years, dogs have faithfully served as man's best friend. Modern dogs descend from the gray wolf. Early humans realized wolves made good guard animals and hunting companions. Over time, these animals became wildly popular pets.

Today, dogs come in all shapes and sizes. Dog lovers now have more than 400 purebred dogs to choose from. But some people prefer mixed **breeds**, or mutts. For them, mutts make the perfect pets! No matter the mix, all dogs belong to the family **Canidae**.

Mutts belong to the same family as wolves. But, dogs and wolves are quite different. Dogs like to be around people, while wolves shy away from humans.

MUTTS

In the beginning, all dogs were mutts. A mutt is a dog that does not have two purebred parents of the same **breed**.

Over time, people began breeding dogs to strengthen certain skills, such as hunting and guarding. Eventually, dogs began to have specialties. For example, golden retrievers were bred to locate and bring in game during a hunt.

Through careful breeding, early mutts developed into the purebred dogs we know today. There is a wide variety of purebred dogs to choose from. But, most dogs are still mutts.

A purebred dog's gene pool is well documented. Its ancestors are the same breed. And, its **heritage** can be traced back for generations. A mutt has an

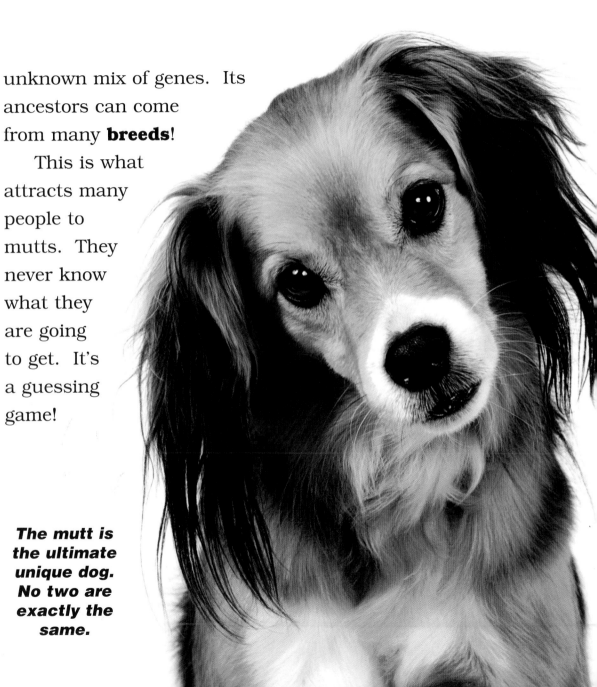

unknown mix of genes. Its ancestors can come from many **breeds**!

This is what attracts many people to mutts. They never know what they are going to get. It's a guessing game!

The mutt is the ultimate unique dog. No two are exactly the same.

What They're Like

The surprise of a mutt's build or look is what many owners love. Personality, size, color, and shape vary from dog to dog. You could wind up owning a dog with a large beagle head on a little dachshund body!

A veterinarian can help determine what **breeds** are in a mutt. This tells an owner what temperament a mutt might have. And, puppy owners can get an idea of what their mutts will look like as adults. However, many owners still end up surprised by the personalities and looks of their mutts.

No one can predict how a mutt will look or act. But you can have fun guessing!

Many people believe mutts are stronger, better tempered, and healthier than purebreds. Some people also think mutts are smarter. However, these claims have not been proven.

COAT AND COLOR

Mutts have a variety of coat types. Their coats depend on the **breeds** in their genes! Mutts can have wavy or straight coats. The hair can be long or short. It may even change as the dogs age.

Some mutts have coats like poodles, so they don't **shed**. Others could have coats like German shepherds. These dogs may shed a lot.

Coat color also varies in mutts. These special dogs come in dozens of colors and patterns. They may have solid white, tan, brown, or black coats. Or, the coats might be a mixture of colors. With more than 400 breeds to mix, the possibilities are endless!

Mutts look like no other dogs. Who can resist these unusual pets?

SIZE

Like its coat type, a mutt's size is also hard to determine when the parent **breeds** are unknown. Mutt sizes range from very small to extra large. A mutt may be tiny like a Pekingese or huge like a Great Dane.

Someone who wants a particular size dog may want to choose an adult mutt. With a mutt puppy, there can be a lot of surprises. You may think you are bringing home a lapdog. But, that lapdog could grow to be the size of a mastiff!

Are you okay with being surprised by your dog's size when it grows up? If so, a mutt might be perfect for you!

13

CARE

No matter their size, all mutts need exercise. The amount of exercise a dog needs depends on its size, age, and energy level. Owners should plan to walk their mutts every day. Some mutts require even more exercise to keep them from growing restless. A bored dog can be a naughty pet!

Some mutts love releasing energy at dog parks.

Just like purebred dogs, grooming needs differ from mutt to mutt. Many mutts simply need

Your mutt needs annual examinations by a veterinarian throughout its life.

regular brushing. Others require professional grooming to keep their coats from becoming **matted**. Mutts also need an occasional bath. And, their nails should be clipped.

A responsible owner must find a good veterinarian to keep his or her mutt healthy. The veterinarian can provide **vaccines**. He or she can also **spay** or **neuter** mutt puppies.

FEEDING

Mutts will eat anything, whether it's good for them or not! However, owners should provide the best-quality dog food they can afford. This will help keep their mutts happy and healthy.

When you buy a mutt, try to find out what it has been eating. Continue that diet to avoid upsetting the dog's stomach. A puppy under six months needs three or four meals a day. By six months of age, it will need only two meals daily.

Dogs must be exercised every day so they don't gain weight. All that exercise makes mutts thirsty! They need a lot of fresh water. Keep a full dish of water next to the dog's food bowl.

Your pet's veterinarian can tell you how much to feed your dog at mealtimes.

THINGS THEY NEED

Mutts love to be around their owners. But, they still need a quiet place to sleep. Soft dog beds or crates are great options. Keep in mind that your mutt may want to sleep in your bedroom.

Many owners prefer to have their mutts living indoors with them. However, many mutts are just as happy outdoors. If your dog lives outside, give it a warm, dry doghouse. A fenced yard will also help keep the dog safe.

Most owners can't play with their dogs constantly. So, they provide their pets with toys to keep them busy. Toys will keep them from chewing your couch or digging up the backyard!

Long walks are perfect for burning up excess energy. Owners need to purchase a leash and a collar for these walks. Some cities also require a license. An identification tag will help someone return your dog to you if it becomes lost.

Walks are a great way to introduce your dog to new people and pets.

PUPPIES

After mating, a female mutt is **pregnant** for about nine weeks. She gives birth to tiny puppies that cannot see or hear. The puppies need their mother to provide food and safety. Dogs are mammals. So, puppies drink milk from their mother.

If you like surprises, a mutt might be the perfect dog for you. There are many places to find these **unique** dogs. Shelters, rescue groups, and newspapers are good resources. Whether choosing a puppy or an adult, make sure the dog looks healthy.

The same day you bring your new pet home, begin some basic training. This will help your mutt grow into a companion you can easily live with. Also, slowly introduce the dog to other pets and people. With lots of love and attention, a mutt can be the perfect family member for 10 to 15 years.

Puppies are cute and full of energy. But, they are a lot of work!

GLOSSARY

breed - a group of animals sharing the same ancestors and appearance. A breeder is a person who raises animals. Raising animals is often called breeding them.

Canidae (KAN-uh-dee) - the scientific Latin name for the dog family. Members of this family are called canids. They include domestic dogs, wolves, jackals, foxes, and coyotes.

heritage - something handed down from one generation to the next.

matted - formed into thick, tangled masses of hair.

neuter (NOO-tuhr) - to remove a male animal's reproductive organs.

pregnant - having one or more babies growing within the body.

shed - to cast off hair, feathers, skin, or other coverings or parts by a natural process.

spay - to remove a female animal's reproductive organs.

unique - being the only one of its kind.

vaccine (vak-SEEN) - a shot given to prevent illness or disease.

WEB SITES

To learn more about mutts, visit ABDO Publishing Company on the World Wide Web at **www.abdopublishing.com**. Web sites about mutts are featured on our Book Links page. These links are routinely monitored and updated to provide the most current information available.

INDEX